— Biomes Atlases —

TROPICAL
FORESTS

Tom Jackson

Raintree

Raintree

www.raintreepublishers.co.uk

Phone 44 (0) 1865 888112
Send a fax to 44 (0) 1865 314091
Visit the Raintree bookshop online at www.raintreepublishers.co.uk
to browse our catalogue and order online.

First published in Great Britain in 2003 by Raintree, Halley Court,
Jordan Hill, Oxford, OX2 8EJ, part of Harcourt Education Ltd.
Raintree is a registered trademark of Harcourt Education Ltd.
Copyright © 2003 The Brown Reference Group plc.
First published in paperback in 2004.
The moral right of the proprieter has been asserted.

Printed and bound in Singapore.

ISBN 1 844 21158 4 (hardback)   ISBN 1 844 21172 X (paperback)
07 06 05 04 03   08 07 06 05 04
10 9 8 7 6 5 4 3 2 1   10 9 8 7 6 5 4 3 2 1

British Library Cataloging-in-Publication Data

A full catalogue is available for this book from the British Library.

The Brown Reference Group plc
Project Editor: Ben Morgan
Deputy Editor: Dr. Rob Houston
Copy-editors: John Farndon and Angela Koo
Consultant: Dr. Mark Hostetler, Department
    of Wildlife Ecology and Conservation,
    University of Florida
Designer: Reg Cox
Cartographers: Mark Walker and
    Darren Awuah
Picture Researcher: Clare Newman
Indexer: Kay Ollerenshaw
Managing Editor: Bridget Giles
Design Manager: Lynne Ross
Production: Alastair Gourlay

Raintree Publishers
Editors: Isabel Thomas and Kate Buckingham

Front cover: Tropical rainforest in northern
Queensland, Australia.
Inset: A sifaka, a type of lemur, Madagascar.

Title page: Banyan tree, Lord Howe Island,
Australia.

The acknowledgments on p. 64 form
part of this copyright page. Every effort has
been made to contact copyright holders of
any material reproduced in this book. Any
omissions will be rectified in subsequent
printings if notice is given to the publishers.

About this book

The introductory pages of this book describe the world's biomes and then the tropical forest biome. The five main chapters look at different aspects of tropical forests: climate, plants, animals, people and future. Between the chapters are detailed maps that focus on key forest areas. The map pages are shown in the contents in italics, *like this*.

Throughout the book you'll also find boxed stories or fact files about tropical forests. The icons here show what the boxes are about. At the end of the book is a glossary, which explains what all the difficult words mean. After the glossary is a list of books and websites for further research and an index, allowing you to locate subjects anywhere in the book.

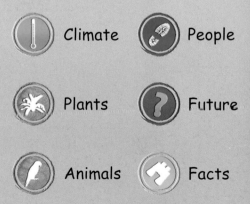

Climate

People

Plants

Future

Animals

Facts

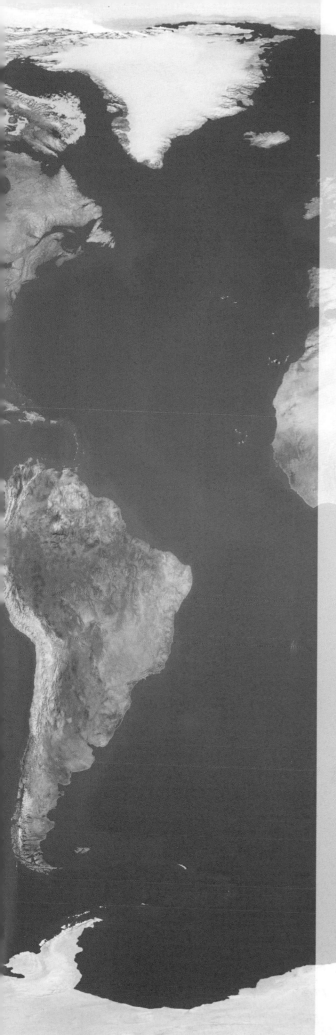

Contents

Biomes of the world

Biologists divide the living world into major zones called biomes. Each biome has its own distinctive climate, plants and animals.

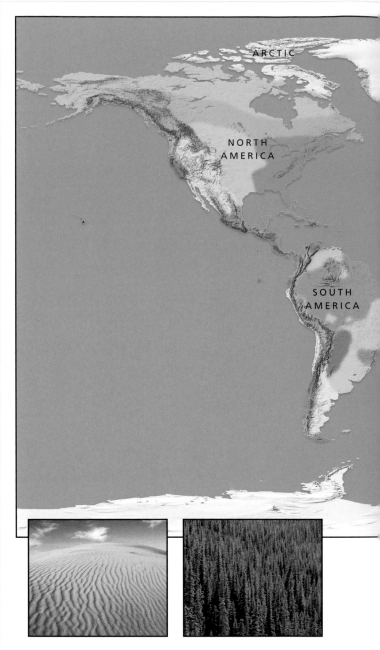

If you were to walk all the way from the north of Canada to the Amazon **rainforest**, you'd notice the wilderness changing dramatically along the way.

Northern Canada is a freezing and barren place without trees, where only tiny brownish-green plants can survive in the icy ground. But trudge south for long enough and you enter a magical world of conifer forests, where moose, caribou (reindeer) and wolves live. After several weeks, the conifers disappear, and you reach the grass-covered prairies of the central USA. The further south you go, the drier the land gets and the hotter the sun feels, until you find yourself hiking through a cactus-filled desert. But once you reach southern Mexico, the cacti start to disappear, and strange **tropical** trees begin to take their place. Here, the muggy air is filled with the calls of exotic birds and the drone of tropical insects. Finally, in Colombia you cross the Andes mountain range – whose chilly peaks remind you a little of your starting point – and descend into the dense, swampy jungles of the Amazon rainforest.

Desert is the driest biome. There are hot deserts and cold ones.

Taiga is made up of conifer trees that can survive freezing winters.

Scientists have a special name for the different regions – such as desert, tropical rainforest and prairie – that you'd pass through on such a journey. They call them **biomes**. Everywhere on Earth can be classified as being in one biome or another, and the same biome often appears in lots of

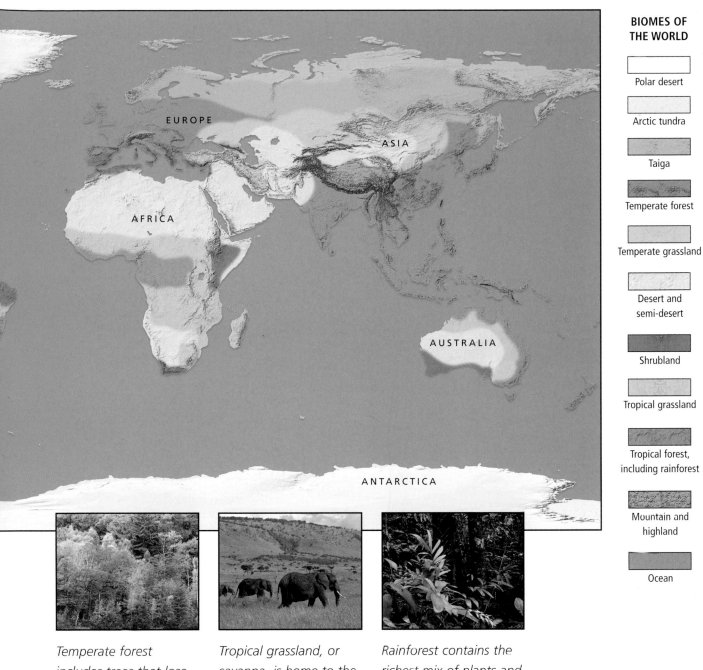

BIOMES OF THE WORLD

Polar desert

Arctic tundra

Taiga

Temperate forest

Temperate grassland

Desert and semi-desert

Shrubland

Tropical grassland

Tropical forest, including rainforest

Mountain and highland

Ocean

EUROPE

ASIA

AFRICA

AUSTRALIA

ANTARCTICA

Temperate forest includes trees that lose their leaves in autumn.

Tropical grassland, or savanna, is home to the biggest land animals.

Rainforest contains the richest mix of plants and animals on the planet.

different places. For instance, there are areas of rainforest as far apart as Brazil, Africa and South-east Asia. Although the plants and animals that inhabit these forests are different, they live in similar ways. Likewise, the prairies of North America are part of the grassland biome, which also occurs in China, Australia and Argentina. Wherever there are grasslands, there are grazing animals that feed on the grass, as well as large carnivores that hunt and kill the grazers.

The map on this page shows how the world's major biomes fit together to make up the biosphere – the zone of life on Earth.

Tropical forests of the world

Tropical forests are dark and humid, filled with tall trees and amazing animals. They grow only in parts of the world that are warm all year: the tropics.

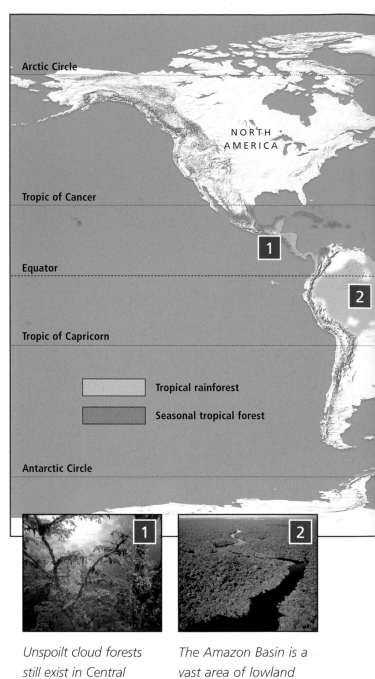

Arctic Circle

NORTH AMERICA

Tropic of Cancer

1

Equator

2

Tropic of Capricorn

◻ Tropical rainforest

◻ Seasonal tropical forest

Antarctic Circle

Unspoilt cloud forests still exist in Central America's mountains.

The Amazon Basin is a vast area of lowland rainforest and rivers.

The best-known type of **tropical forest** is tropical rainforest, which flourishes in places that are both warm and rainy throughout the year. This kind of weather is perfect for plants, allowing them to keep their leaves and grow continuously, instead of dying or shedding their leaves in winter. Tropical rainforests are home to more plant **species** than any other biome – and they contain so many animal species that no one has even tried to count them. The biggest areas of tropical rainforest are in northern South America, central Africa and South-east Asia. There are also small patches of rainforest on rainy mountains, islands and coasts throughout the tropics.

Most parts of the tropics have one or more wet seasons followed by a period of weeks or months when it hardly rains. Rainforests do not usually grow in places with a long dry season, but other types of tropical forest do. There are fewer tree species in these seasonal

tropical forests, but the wildlife is still very rich. In some places the trees are **deciduous** – they shed their leaves for part of the year.

Not all rainforests grow in the tropics. Some forests in **temperate** (cool) countries are also called rainforests. There are temperate rainforests in very rainy parts

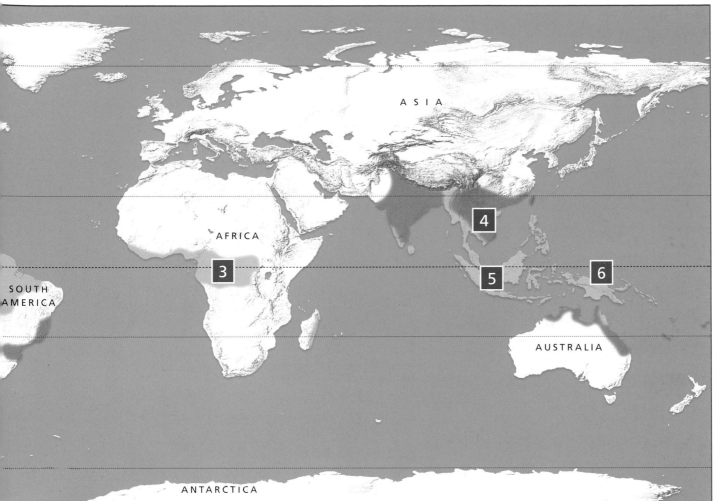

ASIA

AFRICA

3

SOUTH
AMERICA

4

5

6

AUSTRALIA

ANTARCTICA

3

Gorillas and elephants are among the secretive animals of Congo.

4

Seasonal tropical forest surrounds the ancient temples of Cambodia.

5

South-east Asia's rain-forests are home to the world's biggest flowers.

6

Waterfalls cascade from the densely forested slopes of New Guinea.

of Australia, New Zealand, South America and North America. You can find out more about these forests in the *Taiga* and *Temperate Forests* books in this series.

Tropical forests have existed for more than 100 million years. Because they are so ancient, millions of species of plants and

animals have evolved within them, and these species rely on each other in complex ways. As a result, tropical forests are fragile places. Since people started cutting down trees and introducing new species from elsewhere, the forests have begun to change, and many of their original inhabitants are dying out.

Central America

Most of Central America's forests have been felled to create farmland. There are still large stretches, however, in the humid lowlands of the east, and pockets of forest protected in the mountains.

Fact file

▲ Dotted through the jungles of Belize, Guatemala and Mexico are ancient pyramids – temples built by the Mayan people more than 1000 years ago.

▲ Central America is prone to hurricanes. One of the worst was Hurricane Mitch, which in 1998 killed more than 10,000 people.

▲ The roaring cry of the howler monkey carries for miles through Central American forests.

1. Veracruz
The forest in this Mexican state is the most northerly moist tropical forest in the Americas. It is home to howler monkeys, kinkajous, agoutis and pacas.

2. Petén
Guatemala's flat northern province is an unbroken sea of moist tropical forest. Flocks of endangered scarlet macaws squawk in the canopy, while ruined Mayan cities lie hidden below in the undergrowth.

3. Yucatán Peninsula
A flat area with patches of dry tropical forest and filled with cenotes (natural wells) and lagoons. Yucatán was central to the Mayan civilization.

4. Tikal
One of the largest ruined Mayan cities. It reached its peak in the 9th century AD.

5. Cockscombe Basin Jaguar Reserve
Nestled in the Maya Mountains and administered by the local Mayan people, this reserve was designed to be big enough to protect a population of jaguars.

6. Monteverde Cloud Forest
This beautifully lush cloud forest on a volcano in Costa Rica is one of Central America's top attractions for ecotourists.

7. Reserva Biologica Absoluta de Cabo Blanco
One of several reserves in Costa Rica, it was set up to protect both coastal waters and tropical forest.

8. Mosquito Coast
A region still completely covered by swampy forest.

9. Chirripo Grande
On a clear day, you can see both the east and west coasts of Central America from the summit of this mountain.

10. Darien Gap
The Pan-American Highway would join Alaska to southern Chile were it not for this 110-km (70-mile) stretch of jungle. The Darien Gap includes national parks in both Panama and Colombia, and is a useful barrier that stops livestock diseases from passing between North and South America.

Some Central American countries are protecting their remaining forests in reserves, such as the Cordillera Volcanica Central Biosphere Reserve in Costa Rica.

Resplendent quetzals

Quetzals are brilliantly coloured birds that live in the forests of Central America. There are four species, and the aptly named resplendent quetzal is the most spectacular. The male (left) has vivid red and green plumage and a tail up to 1 metre (3 ft) long. Chiefs of the ancient Mayan civilization wore quetzal tail feathers as a sign of their authority. The resplendent quetzal lives only in the Guatemalan highlands, and the bird is still the national symbol of Guatemala, where even the currency is called a quetzal.

Tropical forest climate

Tropical forests grow in parts of the world that are warm all year round and get lots of rain.

Tropical forests are warm because of their position on the Earth's surface. They grow in the region around the **equator** – the imaginary line that divides the Earth into northern and southern halves. In places close to the equator, the sun shines down from high overhead in the middle of the sky for most of the day. However, in places far to the north and south of the equator, the sun stays closer to the horizon (where the ground meets the sky), especially in the winter. You might notice this when you make a long

Rolling hills in the south-eastern part of the Amazon rainforest trap banks of fog in the early mornings. The air here is humid for most of the year.

Small patches of tropical forest flourish on islands throughout the tropics, like this one in the Pacific. The warm sea makes the air humid (moist), creating frequent rain.

Driven by the sun's heat, the humid air over the tropics rises high into the atmosphere. As the rising air cools, the moisture it carries condenses and forms clouds.

Fact file

▲ Enough rain falls on the Amazon rainforest in a year to fill 2000 million Olympic swimming pools.

▲ Tropical forest can soak up heavy rain, preventing floods. In Bangladesh, people have cut down so much forest for fuel or to make money that the country suffers devastating floods every few years.

▲ Scientists have found that during droughts smoke from forest fires stops rain clouds from forming, making the land even drier.

journey from north to south. For example, the Mediterranean is usually sunnier and warmer than Scotland!

To the north and south of the equator are two more imaginary lines: the **tropic of Cancer** to the north and the **tropic of Capricorn** to the south. These lines mark the limit of the region around the equator in which the sun is high in the sky all year round. The area between the two lines is described as the tropics, and things that live there are tropical. In the tropics, the days are more or less the same length all year around, while away from these areas, days are long in summer and short in winter

Invisible water

The effect of the sun being high in the sky is that more heat reaches tropical regions than cooler areas to the north and south. The sun beating down warms the land, the air and

Right: Hurricane Fran closes in on the USA in 1996. Also called typhoons, hurricanes form over the oceans during the wet season in many parts of the tropics.

Main image: Seen from a space shuttle, vast storm clouds (cumulonimbus) form over southern Brazil. Thunderstorms are very common in the wet tropics.

FLORIDA (USA)

the oceans. When water warms up, it begins to **evaporate** – it turns into an invisible gas, or vapour, that mixes with the air.

When air contains a lot of water vapour, we say it is humid. During a hot bath, the air in a bathroom gets very humid because the hot water produces lots of vapour. The air in tropical rainforests is as humid as that in a bathroom for much of the day. The warmth and humidity can be uncomfortable, making people feel sweaty, hot and tired.

Warm air rises. At the equator, warm air is rising nearly all the time, carrying water vapour high into the sky. As the humid air gets higher, it cools down, which makes the vapour turn back into liquid water. The water forms towering rain clouds and falls to the ground as heavy rain. Often the rain comes in violent storms, followed by periods of calm, sweaty conditions.

Tropical seasons

On average, the Earth's equator gets more strong sunlight than anywhere else, so it is the warmest and most humid part of the planet – and therefore the rainiest. A belt of rainy weather roughly encircles the equator, as the maps on this page show (right).

This rain belt changes position slightly during the year. It moves because the Earth is tilted, which causes the amount of sunlight falling on the tropics to vary during the year. In July the North Pole tilts towards the sun, so the tropic of Cancer gets stronger sunlight than the equator. As a result, the belt of rainy weather moves north a bit. In January the opposite happens: the

South Pole tilts towards the sun, and the tropic of Capricorn gets more sunlight than the equator. So the rain belt moves south.

Places very near the equator stay under the rain belt for most of the year, though there might be a 'dry' season when it rains less

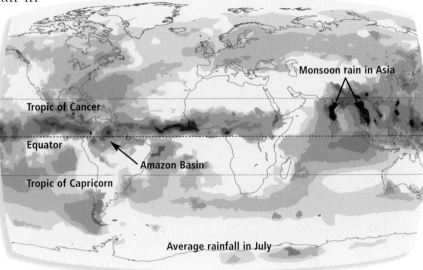

A belt of rainy weather (blue) surrounds the equator. It moves north in summer (above) and south in winter (below), creating wet and dry seasons.

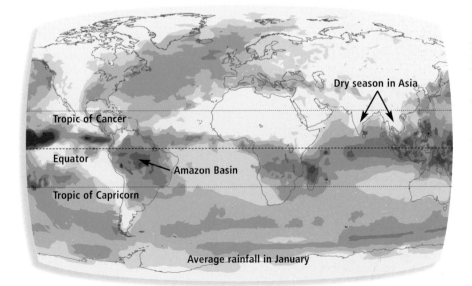

often. These places, such as the Amazon Basin, are where rainforests flourish. As much as 2500 mm (100 in) of rain can fall on a rainforest in an average year – that's five times as much rain as London gets.

 Wildfires

In many parts of the tropics, the rainy season is unreliable. Every few years, the rains fail to fall in large enough quantities, causing a drought. As the forest dries out, the risk of a raging wildfire gets greater and greater. Forest fires can sweep through dry areas of the USA and Australia and burn for weeks on end. In the tropics, they are even worse. In 1998, fire destroyed about 130,000 sq km (50,000 sq miles) of tropical forest worldwide. The smoke blocked out sunlight, and ash covered cities hundreds of kilometres away from the fires.

In contrast, other parts of the tropics move in and out of the rain belt. These places have a significant dry season each year, which has a huge influence on the wildlife.

Places with a very long dry season don't get enough rain for forests. Instead, grass takes over, forming **savanna** (tropical grassland with scattered trees). Places with a shorter dry season have seasonal tropical forests, which are different from rainforests. The trees are shorter, less tightly packed, and many are deciduous – they shed their leaves and stop growing for part of the year.

Monsoons

The biggest area of seasonal tropical forest is in southern Asia. The forest there is called **monsoon** forest because of an unusually intense rainy season termed the monsoon.

The monsoon is caused by a wind that blows in one direction during summer and the opposite way in winter. The summer wind blows north from the Indian Ocean, bringing lots of humidity and rain. This wet season lasts from May to the end of September. The winter wind blows south off Asia and is much drier.

The wind itself is caused by a difference in the way the Earth's land and sea warm up during the year. Land warms up quickly when the summer sun shines on it, but it cools down just as quickly in winter. In contrast, the oceans warm up and cool down slowly.

During summer the vast landmass of Asia warms up enormously because of its size. As a result, air starts rising over it. Moister air from the ocean – the monsoon wind – rushes inland to take the place of the rising air. As it crosses the land, it dumps its moisture as heavy rain. In India it can pour down every day for weeks during the monsoon.

The temple of Angkor Wat in Cambodia, South-east Asia, is surrounded by seasonal tropical forest. The trees are not as tall or densely packed as in a rainforest.

Climographs

Each place in the world has its own pattern of weather. The typical pattern of weather that happens in one place during a year is called climate. We can sum up a place's climate on a climograph, such as the one shown here for St Louis in the USA. The letters along the bottom are the months of the year. The numbers on the left and the small bars show rainfall, and the numbers on the right and the curvy line show temperature. You can see at a glance that St Louis is hottest in July, but December is the driest month.

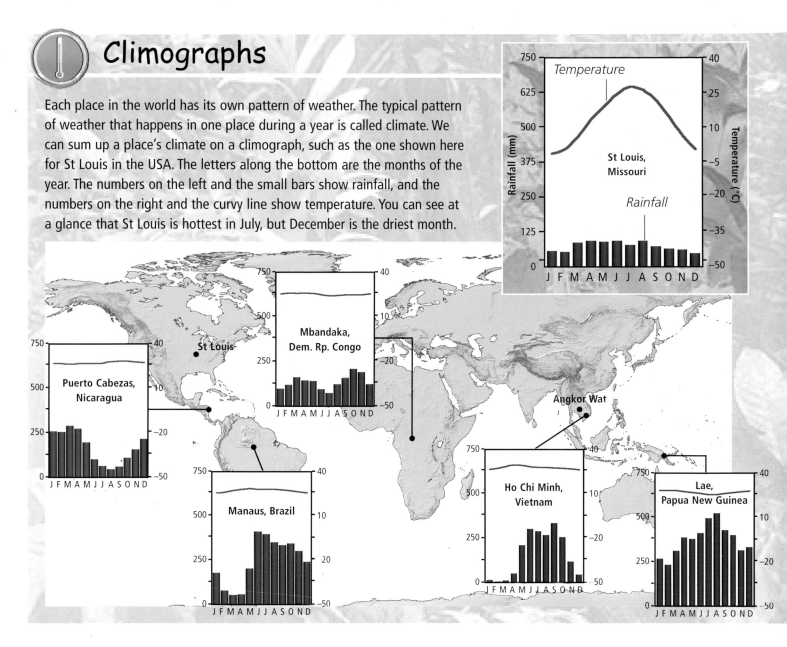

In winter the landmass of Asia cools, and the air above it starts sinking. The sinking air spreads outwards, causing a dry wind to blow south from Asia towards the Indian Ocean. During the dry season, there may be no rain at all for months.

Winds that change direction between seasons in other parts of the world are also called monsoons. The rains that fall on Arizona in the USA in summer are carried by a monsoon wind, for example.

Microclimates

Inside a tropical forest, temperature and humidity vary from place to place. The treetops, for instance, are sunnier and warmer than the forest floor. Scientists call the different conditions found in various parts of the forest 'microclimates'.

Microclimates include more than just temperature and humidity. Light levels, wind speeds and the amounts of the gases **oxygen** and **carbon dioxide** also vary from place to place in the forest. The large range of microhabitats in tropical forests is one of the reasons there are so many species.

Tropical forests do not have summers and winters, but the change in conditions from day to night is almost as great as the change between these two seasons. During the day, it is warm and bright. This is when the plants grow fastest, just as they would in summer.

15

By contrast, the nights are cooler and darker, and most plants do not grow very much, as if it were winter. The difference between the temperatures at night and during the day is larger than the difference between the average temperatures in January and July.

Cloud forests

The weather on mountains is always different from weather in the lowlands. In the tropics, the lowlands are often hot and humid, with little breeze. Mountains are usually cooler and windier, making the air feel fresher. On a single mountain, the weather can vary a great deal – one side might be wet and rainy, while the other is as dry as a desert.

Some tropical mountains always seem to be shrouded in mist, even when the weather below is dry and clear. Strange

Right: Floods are a frequent problem in Chittagong, Bangladesh, during the monsoon season. Deforestation in recent years has made the problem worse.

Under the waterfall

In the heart of southern Africa, the mighty Zambezi River plunges into a gigantic chasm in the ground, forming one of the biggest and most spectacular waterfalls on Earth: Victoria Falls. This breathtaking waterfall is twice as wide and twice as deep as Niagara Falls in North America. Although the land around the waterfall is savanna, patches of rainforest grow on the cliffs around the falls. The forest is watered not by rain but by the constant spray thrown up as the river thunders over the edge.

Many of the animals and plants in this unique microclimate are the same as those found in central Africa's rainforests hundreds of kilometres to the north. There are palms, ebony trees and strangler figs, for example, as well as the magnificent trumpeter hornbill, a fruit-eating bird that also lives in the Congo forests.

and enchanting forests grow in such places, their plants thriving on the moisture-laden air. They are called **cloud forests**.

Cloud forests are as lush and green as lowland rainforests, but the plants are different. The trees are shorter and often crooked. Smaller plants called **epiphytes**, which hang from the trees' branches and cling to their trunks, are much more conspicuous in cloud forests than in lowland rainforests. The epiphytes grow so thickly that the whole forest appears to be dripping with plant life. One of the world's biggest areas of cloud forest is on the Virunga and Ruwenzori mountains of central Africa – home to the endangered mountain gorilla.

At 1430 metres (4700 ft) above sea level, Monteverde cloud forest in Costa Rica is often wrapped in clouds. This reserve is home to more than 400 orchid species.

Amazon rainforest

The Amazon rainforest is as large as all of the USA from the Rockies to the Atlantic Ocean. It occupies a vast, flat river basin filled with branches of the mighty Amazon River.

The mighty rivers of the Amazon Basin flood an area of forest the size of England every rainy season. Birds, monkeys and insects continue life in the canopy, while river dolphins, fish and caimans swim among the tree roots.

Fact file

▲ With few roads, much of the endless Amazon rainforest is inaccessible and unexplored.

▲ Early explorers described it as an area where water and land had swapped places – the wide, smooth rivers are easy to move along, while the dense forest is mostly impassable.

▲ Pico da Neblina, a mountain on the northern edge of the Amazon Basin, is Brazil's highest mountain at 3014 metres (9888 ft) high. It was discovered as recently as 1962.

Slowly but surely

Sloths hang from the branches of trees in the Amazon. They move so slowly that algae (simple plants) grow in their fur, giving the sloths a greenish tinge. Sloths rarely venture to the ground, even giving birth up trees. Their diet of leaves and twigs contains very few nutrients, so they conserve energy by moving very slowly; they spend most of their time hanging motionless while digesting their food. Their hook-like claws are so effective that sloths may stay hanging for weeks after they have died.

Caribbean Sea

Atlantic Ocean

PANAMA

Caracas

TRINIDAD AND TOBAGO

VENEZUELA

NORTH AMERICA

SOUTH AMERICA

Llanos (grassland)

Orinoco River

Mount Roraima

Georgetown

Paramaribo

GUYANA

Cayenne

Bogotá

Canaima National Park

Guiana Highlands

Savanna

SURINAM

FRENCH GUIANA

COLOMBIA

Angel Falls

5

8

0   500   miles

0   500   1000 km

Pico da Neblina

Amazon

9

Central Surinam Nature Reserve

Quito

ECUADOR

Sangay National Park

Putumayo River

Napo River

Japurá River

Negro River

Jaú National Park

6 **7**

Amazon River

Marajó Island

Belém

Equator

Guayaquil

Iquitos

Rio Abiseo National Park

Ucayali River

Flooded forest

Manaus

Madeira River

Tapajós River

Fortaleza

1 **2**

3

Juruá River

Flooded forest

Purus River

Basin

Xingu River

Araguaia River

Tocantins River

(grassland)

Brazilian Highlands

Trujillo

PERU

Manu National Park

4

B R A Z I L

São Francisco River

Salvador

Lima

1

Madidi National Park

Cerrado

Atlantic Forest

N

Andes

BOLIVIA

Mato Grosso Plateau

Brasília

Goiânia

Pacific Ocean

La Paz

Noel Kempff Mercado National Park

Pantanal (wetland)

1

10

1. Andes
Many of the region's rivers begin in the Andes mountains and flow east into the vast Amazon Basin.

2. Rio Abiseo National Park, Peru
These rugged, forested river valleys in the Andean foothills are the last refuge of the yellow-tailed woolly monkey, previously thought extinct, and the tiny mouse opossum.

3. Flooded forest
On the flat bottom of the Amazon Basin, the rivers flood huge areas of nearby forest to a depth of up to 10 m (30 ft).

4. Madidi National Park
The local people take tourists through the forest here to see monkeys and macaws.

5. Angel Falls
The world's highest waterfall tumbles off the sheer side of a table mountain and plummets into the jungle below.

6. Manaus
A large city in the centre of the Amazon rainforest. Manaus was originally the centre of the Brazilian rubber industry.

7. Amazon River
Earth's largest river flows through the heart of the forest.

8. Guiana Highlands
The forests on these low mountains remain pristine, safe from loggers because the area is so difficult to get to.

9. Central Surinam Nature Reserve
An undeveloped hilly area where animals such as jaguars, giant armadillos, tapirs and sloths are protected, as well as 400 species of birds and 8 species of monkeys.

10. Belém
A large port at the mouth of the Amazon, where the river meets the ocean, 6400 km (4000 miles) from the source.

Plants of the forest

The tropical climate is ideal for plants, but life is still tough. Forest plants are crowded together and battle with each other to survive.

Right: Sunlight breaks through the canopy of a tropical rainforest in northern Australia. Rainforest plants grow so densely that little light reaches the forest floor.

The number of plants in a tropical rainforest is staggering. Plants don't just grow from the soil – they also grow on the trees, and a few tiny ones even grow on the plants that are growing on the trees. Most plants grow well when they have plenty of sunlight, lots of water and a warm climate. Tropical rainforests are like this all year round – that's why so many plants grow in them.

Epiphytes are plants that grow on other plants. They get all their moisture from the air or rain.

Getting light
Trees are the kings of the forest, and other plants have to live in their shadow. Many rainforest trees are among the tallest plants in the world – the klinki pine of New Guinea grows to 100 metres (300 ft), almost as tall as St Paul's Cathedral. Trees win the battle for light by growing above the other plants. Unlike the trees you might see in your park, rainforest trees typically have tall trunks with few low branches. At the top, a mass of branches spreads out into a broad crown. Together, all the crowns form a thick layer of leaves called the **canopy**, which soaks up the sun's rays. A few giant trees, called emergents, are taller than the canopy and poke out of the top. Like many rainforest trees, emergents often have buttress roots – huge, spreading roots that grow out from the base of the trunk and support the tree's weight (*see* page 24).

Underneath the canopy it is much darker, but many plants manage to survive in this shady world. Some, like ferns, simply make do with the weak, greenish light that filters through the canopy. Others are cheats – they hitch a ride on other plants.

Hitching a ride
Plants that grow on other plants are called **epiphytes**. They sprout and take root in nooks and crannies on the trunks and branches of trees, where they are much closer to the light than plants of the forest floor are.

Some epiphytes sprout in the canopy, but others climb to get there. The roots of such epiphytes stick to bark, and the plant grows steadily toward the light. As the ends of the roots die away, the whole plant creeps gradually up the tree, like a very slow snail.

Other climbers, such as lianas, start from the ground but lean on a tree for support. With no need to produce a trunk of their own, their wiry stems quickly shoot up to the canopy. Once there, they grow a crown that can be as big as that of the supporting tree, throwing it into shade and weakening it.

Lianas can grow hundreds of metres long in tropical rainforests. As they tangle their way through the canopy, they tie lots of trees

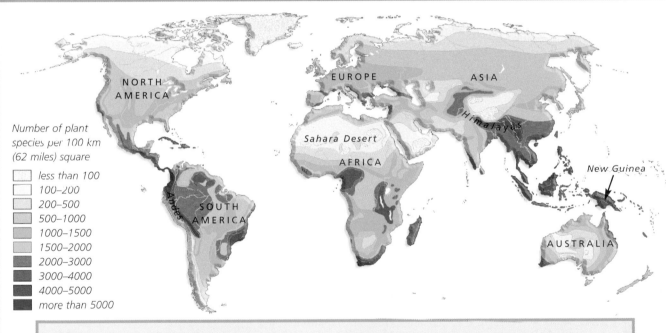

Number of plant
species per 100 km
(62 miles) square

- [ ] less than 100
- [ ] 100–200
- [ ] 200–500
- [ ] 500–1000
- [ ] 1000–1500
- [ ] 1500–2000
- [ ] 2000–3000
- [ ] 3000–4000
- [ ] 4000–5000
- [ ] more than 5000

NORTH AMERICA

EUROPE

ASIA

Himalayas

Sahara Desert

AFRICA

New Guinea

Andes

SOUTH AMERICA

AUSTRALIA

Forest hot spots

The colours on this map show how many plant species there are in different parts of the world. Red and pink places have the most plant species, while yellow areas have the fewest.

You can see at a glance that tropical forests contain some of the richest areas of plant life on Earth, with far more species than deserts or the forests of Europe or North America. The areas with the greatest diversity of plants are where tropical forests meet mountains, such as the Andes in South America, the Himalayas in Asia or the mountains of New Guinea.

Mountains are very diverse habitats, with complex weather and different plants and animals living at varying heights. That's why they support such a variety of species.

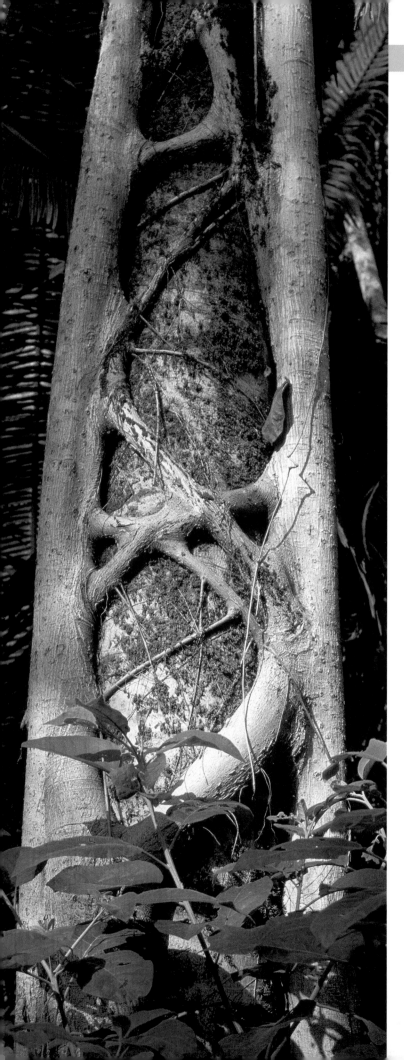

In autumn in Europe, forests turn gold and red as the leaves die. In some tropical forests, the opposite happens: leaves start off red and turn greener as they age. The reasons for the colour changes are similar. Young tropical leaves are often red because they don't have chlorophyll – the green substance that plants use to trap light energy for photosynthesis (making food). Chlorophyll is valuable to plants, but young leaves are the favourite food of many animals and likely to be eaten. So chlorophyll enters the leaves only when they begin to mature. In Europe, forests turn red because the trees extract the chlorophyll before letting the leaves die and fall.

together. They are especially common in open areas, such as riverbanks. People sometimes use lianas as a source of water – they chop them open with a machete and drink the clear water that dribbles out.

Stranglehold

Strangler figs are climbing plants that kill the trees they grow on. They start life as epiphytes growing from seeds left high in the branches by an animal. As a strangler's leaves climb up toward the light, its roots grow down to the ground and wrap around the tree's trunk. As the strangler gets bigger, more roots twist around the trunk, surrounding it with a lattice of roots that appears to be strangling the tree within. Meanwhile, the strangler's crown grows so big that it casts a shadow over the tree, killing it. The tree's trunk eventually rots away, but the strangler stays standing. Its network of roots now form a hollow trunk that is strong enough to hold up the mature crown.

A strangler fig chokes its victim in a Belize rainforest. The tree inside will die and rot away, leaving a hollow.

Lianas provide a handy means of getting around the rainforests of Sumatra. Despite their agility, orangutans suffer many falls from the trees.

Water, water everywhere

For plants in many biomes, getting water is often a challenge. But for the trees in a rainforest, the problem is sometimes the opposite – they have to cope with frequent downpours. If too much water collects on the leaves, it weighs down the branches or causes mould to grow. So, many rainforest trees have smooth leaves that repel water and pointed leaf tips that help water dribble off.

Plants get water through their roots. Though rainforest trees are huge, their roots are mostly less than 60 cm (2 ft) deep – much shallower than the roots of temperate-forest trees. Because of the shallow roots, rainforest trees are prone to fall over in storms, so some have stilt-like roots that prop them up. The buttress roots of emergents also help them withstand storms. Although shallow, the roots of rainforest trees often spread very widely from the base of the tree.

Up in the air

Epiphytes don't start life on the ground, so they have to get their water elsewhere. Many have roots that collect rain dribbling down the tree, and many can absorb water from the humid air. Most epiphytes have thick, leathery leaves or swollen stems that store water. Some, called tank bromeliads, collect water in a tiny pond. Tank bromeliads have a rosette of spiky leaves like the cluster of leaves on a pineapple. The leaf bases overlap,

This tropical mistletoe is a parasite. It grows on trees and has roots that burrow into its host to steal water and nutrients.

forming a bowl that traps rainwater. Some frogs lay their eggs in these bromeliad ponds, and the tadpoles develop inside them.

Some epiphytes are **parasites** – they steal food and water from another plant. Parasitic epiphytes drive their roots into the host tree to tap into its veins. Some parasites have their own leaves for making food, as well.

Getting nutrients

Plants don't just need water and light to survive – they also need chemicals called **nutrients**, which they get from rotting animal and plant remains in the soil. The soil in a tropical forest forms from animal droppings, dead leaves, fragments of wood and dead animals. Fungi, bacteria and insects break this mixture down, turning it into a damp compost and releasing the nutrients. Because tropical forests are often warm and wet, the rotting matter breaks down very quickly, and the trees absorb the nutrients almost as soon as they are released. As a result, the soil in a tropical forest is surprisingly shallow and low in nutrients – temperate forests have much thicker, richer soil. If rotting matter was not constantly replacing nutrients, the soil would soon run out of them and nothing would grow.

Epiphytes somehow have to get nutrients from high in the trees. Some collect falling bits of debris, which slowly build up into a thin layer of soil. Those that steal water from their host tree get a free supply of nutrients dissolved in the water.

Buttress roots give rainforest trees extra support. Because rainforests have shallow soil, most trees have wide, spreading roots rather than deep ones.

Chemical war

If you think a rainforest is living banquet, full of tasty leaves for plant-eating animals, then think again. Many of the leaves contain deadly poisons or foul-tasting chemicals that stop animals from eating them. Leaf-eating monkeys get around this problem, but it takes effort. They choose only the youngest, most tender leaves, and they eat leaves from lots of different tree species. By varying their diet, they prevent any single poison from building up too much.

Flower power

Flowers are not just for decoration – they enable plants to reproduce sexually. Flowers produce male cells and female cells. When a male cell from one flower joins with a female cell from another flower, the united cells grow into an embryo (the beginning of a new plant), and a **seed** forms around this.

This might sound straightforward, but there's a snag: unlike animals, plants can't move around to find a mate. They have other ways of making sure that male and female cells from different plants join together. The most common solution is to make **pollen**, a dust-like substance that carries the male cells from one flower to another. When pollen lands on the female part of a flower, it sprouts and grows down into the flower to deliver the male cell. This process is termed **pollination**.

Finding a partner

Pollination is tricky in tropical forests because there are so many different species. A plant can reproduce only with other members of its species, but the nearest mate may be miles away. Among many of the tall tree species, the wind carries pollen. The trees' flowers release vast amounts of tiny pollen grains into the air. Most blow away and get lost, but a few grains settle on exactly the right flowers somewhere else in the forest.

Beneath the canopy, the air is too still for wind pollination. Instead, flying animals carry the pollen between flowers. In return for this service, the animals receive **nectar**, a sugary liquid produced by flowers. A few animals also eat some of the pollen.

Red-eyed tree frogs clamber over a Heliconia *plant in Belize.* Heliconia *flowers are usually pollinated by hummingbirds.*

Getting noticed

Flying insects, such as bees, beetles, butterflies and moths, are the most common animal pollinators. Many flowers have a specific shape that suits a certain type of pollinator. For example, flowers that beetles pollinate are broad and dish-shaped, allowing these large insects to scramble about as they gather nectar. As they do so, pollen sticks to them, ready to rub off on the next flower.

Bee flowers open during the day, when bees are busiest. Such flowers are often brightly coloured, with lines that direct the bee towards the pollen. Butterfly flowers are usually funnel-shaped. To reach the nectar at the base of the funnel, a butterfly uses a very long mouthpart that works like a straw. When the butterfly isn't feeding, the mouthpart coils up under its head. Moths feed like butterflies, but at night. Their flowers are often white and scented so they are easy to find in the dark.

Some flowers are pollinated by birds and bats. Bird flowers are usually red and are tough because birds are much larger than

Banana flowers are pollinated by bats. Wild banana plants produce fruit and seeds after pollination, but cultivated banana plants (right) produce seedless fruit.

insects. Hummingbirds hover beside their flowers, flapping their wings up to seventy times a second to keep perfectly still while they probe for nectar with their bills. Bats feed at night, so their flowers are often pale, with a musty scent. Most bat flowers look a little like brushes – when a bat pays a visit, the brush gives its chest a dusting of pollen.

Many birds and bats are too big to fly into the middle of a plant, so their flowers are usually positioned on the outside of the plant. Banana flowers are like this and are usually pollinated by bats.

Spreading out

Once a plant has produced its seeds, it can't just drop them onto the ground. If they sprouted there and started growing, the young plants would end up crowded together, competing with each other and their parent for light, nutrients and water. Most plants, therefore, have ways of dispersing their seeds. Although many go to waste in the crowded forest, a few stand a good chance of finding just the right place to start life.

Many of the tallest trees produce seeds with wings, which make the seeds spin around in the air, slowing their fall. When such seeds are released from the high treetops, they can travel a long way on the breeze. However, most tropical forest plants have a different strategy to spread their seeds: they bribe animals to carry the seeds away.

The usual way of doing this is by enclosing the seed in an edible fruit. Animals eat the fruit, swallow the seeds and move off into the forest. When the seeds eventually pass out of the animal's body, they are far from the parent plant. They land on the ground in a heap of droppings – a perfect fertilizer for the young plants.

A snowcap hummingbird hovers over a wild poinsettia flower to sip nectar. This tiny bird from Central America is a mere 6 cm (2.5 in) long – people often mistake it for an insect.

Biggest flower in the world

The world's biggest flower belongs to a peculiar plant called *Rafflesia arnoldii*, which grows only in the rainforests of Sumatra. In some ways *Rafflesia* is more like a fungus than a plant. It has no true roots, stems or leaves, and it cannot make its own food. Instead, it lives as a parasite, sending fine, thread-like growths into vines to steal water and nutrients. The only part of *Rafflesia arnoldii* that you can see is its gigantic red and white flower, which grows to 1 metre (3 ft) wide on the forest floor. Even the flower is weird. It smells of rotting flesh, attracting flies that normally lay eggs on dead animals. Tricked by the foul stench, the flies unwittingly pollinate the flower.

sucking
mouthpart

*Above: With its slender mouthpart unrolled, a postman
butterfly sucks nectar from a flower in Costa Rica.*

In temperate climates, plants that produce
fruit or nuts all tend to do so at the end of
summer. In a tropical rainforest, different
types of fruit come into season at different
times of the year. Because fruit and nuts are
usually available somewhere in the forest,
many animals specialize in eating little else.
They include fruit bats, many monkeys and
birds such as parrots, toucans and hornbills.
Such animals usually move around a lot as
they search for the few trees with ripe fruit.

Stinky fruit

Durians are large, spiky fruits that look like
giant horse chestnuts. Although the flesh
inside a durian is sweet, the fruit has such a
disgusting, rotten smell that it is banned from
many restaurants in South-east Asia, where
durian trees grow. However, in the forest, the
powerful smell attracts orangutans, tigers and
many other animals, all of which eagerly
devour the custard-like flesh.

Above: Durians smell revolting to us, but many animals, from orangutans to tigers, find them delicious.

Awaiting the gap

Once a seed has been carried across the forest, dropped in a perfect patch of soil and sprouted into a sapling (baby tree), it faces a new challenge: lack of light. The floor of a tropical forest is usually dark and gloomy, so how can a sapling get the light it needs to grow all the way to the canopy?

For many trees, the answer is to wait. After reaching a few metres tall, the saplings stop growing. They can wait for years like this, absorbing just enough energy from the dim light to keep themselves alive. Their big chance comes when a large tree falls down, creating a gap in the canopy that lets sunlight flood onto the forest floor.

Once a gap opens, the saplings race upwards in a fierce contest to fill the empty space. Eventually, one wins, and the gap disappears. Some small plants grow only in gaps. They flower and set seed quickly, before the forest closes in again, and their seeds lie ready in the soil for the next gap to form.

Banyan trees

Producing seeds enables trees to spread to new places, but some tropical trees can spread where they stand – by growing sideways. The banyan tree, a native of tropical Asia, produces aerial roots that grow down from its branches. When they reach the ground, they become new trunks. A single banyan tree can spread indefinitely this way, turning into a thicket or even a small forest. One banyan tree in Hawaii covers nearly half a hectare (about an acre).

Congo rainforest

The Congo rainforest lies in a vast river basin straddling the equator in central Africa. The heart of the forest is a largely unspoiled wilderness, where only rivers and occasional clearings break the canopy.

The swampy clearings, or bais, of the Congo region are like magnets to wildlife. Animals such as forest elephants and lowland gorillas visit them to eat roots, grass and minerals. The bais allow scientists to study the animals before they melt back into the forest.

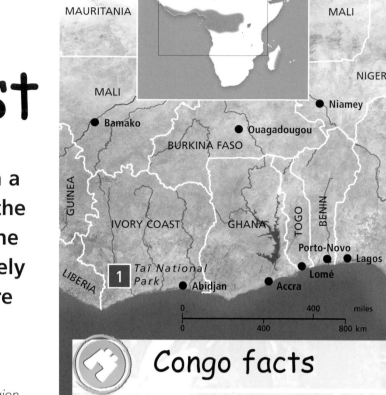

Congo facts

▲ Most of Africa's rainforest is in or around the Congo basin, but there is also rainforest in parts of west Africa, including Liberia and Ivory Coast.

▲ The central part of the Congo rainforest is so swampy and difficult to reach that it remains almost untouched by loggers and farmers.

▲ One of the main threats to the forest wildlife is poaching. Poachers hunt elephants for ivory and gorillas and other animals for meat.

▲ Deforestation by farmers and loggers is a growing problem in outer parts of the Congo basin.

▲ The Bronx Zoo in New York in the USA houses a 2-hectare (about 6 acres) reconstruction of Congo rainforest, complete with 22 gorillas, 11 waterfalls and 15,000 plants of nearly 400 species.

1. Taï National Park
One of the last major remnants of primary tropical rainforest in west Africa. Its chimpanzees use rocks as tools to open oil-palm nuts.

2. Dja Faunal Reserve
One of the best-protected rainforests in Africa, with 90 per cent of its area undisturbed. The Dja River surrounds it, forming a natural barrier.

3. Congo River
Africa's second-longest river after the Nile.

4. Salonga National Park
The largest rainforest reserve in Africa and one of the largest national parks on Earth, home to forest elephants and bonobos. The park has few human settlements and is accessible only by river.

5. Congo Basin
A vast area of lowland rainforest, swamps and winding rivers. Much of the Congo basin floods in the rainy season.

6. Virunga National Park
One of the last refuges of mountain gorillas, the largest primates in the world. War in neighbouring Rwanda has driven refugees into Virunga, causing deforestation.

7. Ituri Forest
Dramatic scenery and tumbling waterfalls make this hilly corner of the Congo very beautiful. The Ituri Forest is the homeland of the Mbuti people.

8. Okapi Wildlife Reserve
A protected part of Ituri, home to 5000 of the world's 30,000 remaining wild okapis. Okapis are short-necked relatives of giraffes with striped legs.

9. Gombe Stream National Park
A woodland reserve famous for its chimpanzees. Scientists have been studying their complex social behavior for decades.

10. Lake Victoria
Africa's largest lake is the main source of the White Nile, which flows north to the Nile river. The region around Lake Victoria is one of the most densely populated parts of Africa.

Bonobos

One of the Congo rainforest's most interesting animals is the bonobo, or pygmy chimpanzee, which lives only to the south of the Congo River. Despite its name, it is no smaller than its cousin the common chimpanzee.

Scientists think bonobos (right) are descended from a group of chimpanzees that crossed the Congo River from north to south about 1.5 million years ago. Isolated by the river and its swamps, they evolved separately. Common chimpanzees live in aggressive, male-dominated societies. The males form gangs and sometimes wage war on rival groups. In contrast, bonobos live in more peaceful, female-dominated societies. In addition to grooming each other regularly (as most primates do), bonobos use sexual behavior to forge and strengthen social bonds.

31

Animals of the forest

Tropical forests teem with an amazing number of weird and wonderful animals, from flying frogs and birds of paradise to giant millipedes and midget hippos. They are also home to some of the most colourful animals on Earth.

Nobody knows how many animal species live on Earth, but one thing's certain: a lot of them live in tropical forests. One scientist collected beetles from just nineteen trees in the rainforest of Panama. He counted nearly 1000 species, so the total number of tropical beetles worldwide could be millions. Beetles probably outnumber most other animal species, but tropical forests are still home to countless other insects and spiders, not to mention snakes, monkeys, bats, birds, frogs, cats, anteaters and all sorts of animals you've probably never heard of.

Blue-and-yellow macaws are a common sight in the Amazon rainforest. These birds form very strong bonds with each other and are often seen in pairs.

Grasping toes and flexible ankle joints allow kinkajous to hang by their feet while searching for food. They live in Central and South America.

Animal niches

You might wonder how so many species could survive in such a crowded place – surely they'd end up eating each other's food and getting in each other's way? They avoid such problems because each animal species has its own particular way of life, or **niche**. It eats certain foods, lives in a particular part of the forest and uses unique skills to survive.

A niche is not just the animal's home in the forest, such as the canopy or a rotting log. It is a combination of habitat, behaviour and time. For example, an animal that feeds at night has a different niche from one that feeds during the day. Likewise, two species of bats might fly around the same sorts of plants in search of insects to eat, but one might prefer large moths while the other eats flies. Each bat, therefore, has its own niche.

33

Toucans (above) live in South America, while hornbills (right) live in Africa. They have evolved into species that fill similar niches in forests thousands of miles apart.

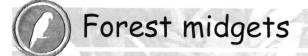

Forest midgets

Many of the mammals that live in tropical forests are smaller than their relatives from more open country. These small animals are often called pygmies.

Africa's Congo rainforest is home to pygmy elephants and pygmy hippos, for example. Pygmy elephants are about half the weight of their savanna cousins, while pygmy hippos are one-tenth the weight of other hippos (but still three times heavier than a person). Rhinoceroses in Asian forests are also much smaller than their grassland relatives in Africa, and deer in some rainforests are as small as rabbits.

One reason forest mammals are small is that it helps them move through undergrowth. Another is that there is more high-energy food, such as fruit, in forests. Small mammals need a constant supply of energy, but larger mammals digest and use their food more slowly. Savanna elephants grow to a huge size while eating large quantities of poor-quality food.

Tropical forests are complex places, with millions of different niches. This is why so many animal species can coexist in them.

Similar but different

Tropical forests in different parts of the world have very different sets of animals, but they often have similar niches. As a result, unrelated animals have become similar through evolution. Scientists call this process convergent evolution.

One example is the similarity of South America's toucans to the hornbills of Africa and Asia. Both types of birds have spectacularly long bills, which they use to break open nuts and fruits.

Another pair of animals that look and behave the same way but live on the opposite sides of the world are the pudu and mouse deer. Pudus live in the forests of South America, where they feed on fruit. They are only 30 cm (1 ft) long – about the same size as rabbits. They share the title of world's smallest deer with mouse deer, which live in the forests of Malaysia. They, too, are no bigger than rabbits and feed on fruit. These

South-east Asia's slow lorises come out at night to look for insects and fruit, using their large eyes to see in the gloom. To avoid being spotted by predators, they do everything in slow motion.

deer species have evolved in similar ways because they occupy similar niches in the rainforest.

Sometimes a niche is filled by a completely different type of animal. For example, there are no monkeys or lemurs in the tropical forests of Australia, so the fruit-eating niche is filled mainly by birds, especially parrots and pigeons.

Monkey business

Monkeys are perhaps the most familiar of forest animals. These agile creatures live all over the forest from the highest branches in the treetops to the forest floor and along the edges of rivers. Monkeys belong to a larger group of animals called **primates**, nearly all of which live in tropical forests. Besides

monkeys, the primate group includes apes, lemurs and smaller animals called bushbabies, tarsiers and lorises. Apes are generally bigger than monkeys, with longer arms and no tails. Gorillas, chimpanzees, orangutans, gibbons and humans are all apes. Lemurs are easy to tell apart from monkeys because they have cat-like faces with long snouts. They live only on the island of Madagascar, where there are no monkeys. Bushbabies, lorises and tarsiers are small, **nocturnal** (night-active) primates with huge eyes for seeing in the dark. While monkeys,

 # Tree kangaroo

Although there are no monkeys in the forests of Australia and New Guinea, other mammals have taken to the trees. One of the most surprising is the tree kangaroo, a relative of the more familiar kangaroos that hop around on the ground. The tree kangaroo has more muscular arms and wider feet than its ground-dwelling cousins. It uses the claws on its hands to grip branches, and it can 'walk' by moving its back legs alternately – something other kangaroos cannot do. It can also hop along the ground when it needs to.

In Central and South America, many of the monkeys have a tail that is prehensile – it can wrap around things and be used as a fifth limb. Spider monkeys (left) have tails strong enough to support their whole body weight. Their prehensile tails help them move, but spider monkeys can also swing from branch to branch like gibbons, using their thumbless hands as hooks.

High-ranking male mandrills have very bright blue and red marks on their face as a display of status. These marks grow darker when a male is spoiling for a fight.

The world's smallest monkey – the pygmy marmoset – weighs a mere 90 g (3 oz) and could sit on your hand. This diminutive primate lives in the northern parts of the Amazon rainforest. While large monkeys swing through the trees, pygmy marmosets are small enough to perch on blades of grass.

apes and lemurs tend to live in social groups, most of the nocturnal primates live on their own or with their offspring.

Large and small

The world's largest monkey is the mandrill, which lives on the floor of Africa's Congo rainforest. A fully grown male mandrill weighs about as much as an eight-year-old child, while females are half the weight of males. Male monkeys are often larger than females because they have to fight with each other to win mates.

Like many primates, mandrills live in social groups with a ranking system. The top-ranking male usually gets more mating opportunities than his rivals in the group.

Only adult males sport the bright markings for which mandrills are famous. Blue and crimson patches of skin on the buttocks complement those on the face.

Above: Lemurs spends most of their time in the trees. Sifakas are lemurs that make spectacular leaps from tree to tree, but their jumping style of movement seems clumsy on the ground.

Below: Pygmy marmosets are the world's smallest monkeys. They are nervous animals and move in a quick, jerky manner. Unlike most monkeys, they have claw-like nails that help them cling to tree trunks.

In all, there are nearly two hundred species of monkeys, the majority of which live in tropical forests. Most eat either fruit or leaves, but a few species, such as capuchins, feed on all sorts of food, from shellfish to insects and small frogs.

Aping about

Many people think apes are large monkeys, but they are different in lots of ways. Apes don't have tails, and while monkeys usually have long back legs and shorter arms, most apes have arms longer than their legs. Monkeys are good at scampering along branches and jumping from tree to tree, but apes climb more slowly, using their strong arms to grip the tree trunk. Gibbons are an exception, though – these apes use their long arms to swing below the branches.

Orangutans are red-haired apes that live on only two islands in South-east Asia. These gentle giants spend their whole lives in the

Getting around

Most mammals get around by walking on all fours, but that's not the best way to travel in a dense rainforest – especially if all the best food is up in the canopy. As a result, all sorts of unusual ways of moving have evolved in forest animals. In a South-east Asian forest, for instance, fruit bats fly, colugos glide, siamang gibbons swing, orangutans clamber lazily through the branches, slow lorises creep very slowly to avoid being seen, squirrels scuttle up and down trunks and langur monkeys make bold leaps between treetops.

Gibbons can move at tremendous speed through the canopy by swinging underhand from branch to branch. Their wrists and shoulders are so flexible that, while hanging from one arm, they can turn up to 360 degrees without having to let go of the branch.

trees – they find it hard to walk on the ground because their feet are turned inwards for holding branches. At night, orangutans weave beds out of twigs and branches high in the trees. The other apes – chimpanzees and gorillas – live in large groups in the forests of Central Africa. They spend most of their time on the ground, though

Gorillas are the largest of the primates. They are highly endangered due to poaching and loss of forest.

they also often sleep in beds woven out of tree branches. Only one species of ape lives outside tropical forests: humans.

Fellow travellers

Primates are by no means the only mammals in tropical forests. Like most other types of forest, tropical forests are also home to all sorts of rodents – animals like mice, rats and squirrels. Most rodents are small, but in South American forests a few species have evolved into giants.

The agouti is a shy, secretive rodent that searches the forest floor for fallen fruit. At 0.6 metres (2 ft) long, it is so big

Agoutis are attracted to the sound of ripe fruit falling on the forest floor. Like squirrels, they bury food in secret stores, helping spread the trees' seeds.

highlands around the Amazon Basin. Unlike their fiercer cousins, tropical bears do not hunt large animals. Instead, they eat a mixed diet of fruit, roots, leaves and insects.

The top **predators** of the forest are the cats. The most famous forest cat is the tiger, which once lived throughout Asia. This wonderful animal is now very rare and survives only in small, protected pockets of forest. Tigers are so big and powerful that they will prey on anything they can catch, even small elephants and rhinoceroses. A few develop a taste for human flesh and become maneaters.

Other forest-dwelling cats include leopards and ocelots, both of which have spots that help them hide in the dappled shade. Leopards are the success story of the cat

that many people mistake it for a small deer. Its relative the capybara is even bigger – it grows to more than 1.2 metres (4 ft) long and can weigh as much as a person, making it the biggest rodent in the world. Capybaras are good swimmers and usually live close to rivers, lakes or marshes. Local people call them water pigs, but they are more closely related to rats than pigs.

Other forest mammals include bears and hoofed animals, such as deer and cattle. Tropical bears are much smaller than the giant hunters of colder areas. Sun bears live in South-east Asian forests; honey bears, named for their favourite food, live in India and Sri Lanka; while spectacled bears live in cool forests in the

Jaguars are often heard but seldom seen in the tropical forests of Latin America. They are solitary animals and often become aggressive when they meet each other.

Few parrots are as colourful as the rainbow lorikeet of eastern and northern Australia. Lorikeets are small parrots with brush-tipped tongues for sipping nectar.

Hello, Polly

Tropical forests can seem like unbroken stretches of green, but there are occasional splashes of colour. Among the most colourful inhabitants are parrots – large, noisy birds that generally have curved beaks for cracking nuts and cutting fruits. Some parrots have magnificent long tails. The largest parrot of all is the hyacinth macaw of Brazil, which measures 1 metre (40 in) from head to tail.

Parrots are often known by different names. Macaws, cockatoos, lorikeets and parakeets are all different types of parrots, for example. Unlike most birds, parrots have two forwards-pointing toes and two backwards-pointing ones. This allows a parrot to lift food to its mouth with one foot while clinging to a branch with the other.

Birds are especially common in the forests of New Guinea and Australia, where there are fewer mammals to compete with.

world. While most big cats have declined in number because of environmental damage, leopards are still relatively common in Africa and Asia. When they make a kill, leopards haul the victim's mutilated body into a tree to hide it from other animals. There are no leopards in South America, but the stockier jaguar fills a similar niche.

 ## Elephant bird

The island of Madagascar used to have some of the most amazing animals in the world – before people arrived and started cutting down the forests. One was the elephant bird, a gigantic, flightless bird nearly twice as tall as a person and weighing 450 kg (1000 lbs). Even the egg of an elephant bird was enormous, as 1000-year-old specimens (right) found buried in sand have proved. Scientists think the elephant bird fed on the bodies of dead animals, and it may have survived on Madagascar until as recently as 1100 years ago. Some Arabic and Persian myths describe a terrifying,

giant bird called the roc. Perhaps these stories were based on reports from merchants who once sailed from Arabia to the waters around Madagascar.

The emerald tree boa hangs from branches in the Amazon, impersonating vines. It kills small animals by wrapping around them and squeezing until they suffocate; then it swallows them whole.

Wriggling reptiles

The largest snakes in the world live in tropical forests. The green anaconda is the heaviest and lives in swampy parts of South America, including the Amazon. The longest snake is the reticulated python, which can reach nearly 10 metres (32 ft). These snakes are just two of thousands of **reptile** species, including geckos, chameleons, monitor lizards, rattlesnakes, vipers, tree pythons and boa constrictors, that live in tropical forests. Snakes that live in trees tend to have long, slender bodies that can drape across flimsy branches without falling through. Geckos have sticky feet that let them run up vertical trunks or even along the bottom of branches. And chameleons have strange, pincer-like feet for gripping branches as they creep along.

The Komodo dragon – a huge, flesh-eating monitor lizard – holds the record for the world's heaviest lizard. It reaches 135 kg (300 lbs) in weight and lives only on several islands in South-east Asia.

New Guinea is home to the birds of paradise. Male birds of paradise are brightly coloured and adorned with wild headdresses and long tails – all to impress the females.

One of the strangest birds in the world lives in the flooded forests of Ecuador and Peru. The hoatzin is known by local people as the stink bird because of its disgusting smell. It looks a little like a turkey, but it has a bright blue face and a punk hairstyle of feathers. What makes this bird unique is that the young chicks have claws on their growing wings, which they use for clinging to trees. This prehistoric feature is probably a leftover from the distant reptilian ancestors that birds evolved from: dinosaurs.

The mangrove snake lives in the forests and swamps of South-east Asia. It sniffs out prey with its tongue and kills with a venomous bite.

Left: The strawberry poison-dart frogs of Central America are tiny, growing to only 2.5 cm (1 in) long. To attract females, males inflate their throats and make a trilling sound. The tadpoles develop in puddles or pools of water in bromeliad plants.

Wet and wild

Amphibians are animals such as frogs, toads and salamanders that live partly in water and partly on land. They need to keep their skin moist when they are out of water, so the damp climate of a rainforest is perfect for them. The many pools, puddles and slow-flowing rivers provide countless sites for the tadpoles to develop.

Below: Yellow-banded poison frogs live in Colombia and Venezuela. Their skin contains a potent nerve toxin derived from the ants they eat.

Frogs are so common in rainforests that their strange calls, which range from croaks to bleeps, often fill the air at night. Some tropical frogs have beautiful skin colours and patterns that warn predators that they are poisonous. The poison-dart frogs of the Amazon

Right: Red-eyed tree frogs hide in the trees of Central America during daylight hours, using sticky toe tips to hold on. Their amazing eyes perhaps serve to startle any predators that wake them.

have the most spectacular colours, but also the most deadly poison. The most dangerous species is the terrible poison-dart frog of western Colombia – a single lick of its skin can kill you. Forest people use the skin of this frog to poison their arrow tips for hunting.

Other amazing forest frogs include the tree frogs, which have sticky disks on their toes that help them cling to leaves and branches. Some tree

Right: Blue poison frogs live only in southern Surinam. They are ravenous eaters, preying on fruit flies, termites, crickets and ants. Their striking colour has made them popular pets – many are now bred in captivity.

Wallace's flying frogs use their webbed feet and skin flaps between their legs to glide up to 15 metres (50 ft) between trees in the forests of Borneo.

frogs lay their eggs in trees, gluing them to the undersides of leaves overhanging water. When the tadpoles have developed, they drop into the water below. Flying frogs are tree frogs with webbed feet and skin flaps that act like wings, enabling them to glide great distances after leaping from a tree.

Leaf-cutter ants use leaf cuttings to grow an edible fungus inside their nests. The ants consume more plant matter than any other group of animals in the forests of Central and South America.

Insects and spiders

Large animals might be exciting to spot, but they are insignificant in number compared to the insects and other **invertebrates** that teem over every surface in a tropical forest.

Forest insects range from huge, spike-covered crickets to shiny beetles that appear to be made of metal. There are tiny wasps that live inside plants, butterflies bigger than your hand and all sorts of insects disguised as twigs, leaves, thorns or flecks of dirt. The wandering spiders of Brazil are perhaps the world's most dangerous spiders. These aggressive creatures wander into houses and attack people with little provocation – and a single bite can kill.

Tropical forests are home to the world's biggest insects. Top prize for the heaviest insect goes to the goliath beetle of Africa's Congo rainforest. It grows to 11 cm (4.3 in) long and reaches 100 g (3.5 oz) in weight. The longest insect is *Pharnacia*

Below: Goliath beetles of Africa are the world's heaviest insects. When they are in flight they sound like miniature helicopters.

Each leg ends in a pair of claws, or tarsi, used for gripping tree trunks or other surfaces.

Male goliaths have horns for fighting.

ACTUAL SIZE

wing case

When the wings are not in use, they fold away under protective wing cases.

Wallace's Line

PHILIPPINES

BRUNEI

MALAYSIA

Borneo

Sulawesi

Wallace's Line

Pacific Ocean

New Guinea

PAPUA NEW GUINEA

INDONESIA

Sumatra

Indian Ocean

Java

Bali

Lombok

EAST TIMOR

N

| 0 | | 500 | miles |
| 0 | 500 | 1000 km | |

AUSTRALIA

If you walked in the footsteps of the explorers and naturalists of the 19th century, through the forests of Malaysia and across to the islands of Indonesia, you might notice changes in the animals around you. You would leave behind the familiar animals such as deer, monkeys and cats as you left the shores of Bali or Borneo. In Sulawesi and Lombok you would see a mixture of animals from Asia and Australia, but eventually, if you reached New Guinea and Australia, you would see mainly the marsupial mammals that live there, such as tree kangaroos, possums and pademelons, a type of wallaby. The famous naturalist Alfred Russel Wallace (1823–1913) drew an imaginary line that divided these characteristic animals of Asia and Australia.

Clouded leopard

Sambar

Rhesus macaque

Pademelon

Tree kangaroo

Bird of paradise

Striped possum

serratipes, a stick insect from Malaysia that reaches 55.5 cm (22 in) in length – as long as a man's arm.

The leaf litter on the forest floor is alive with tiny animals. Industrious termites and ants play a largely unseen role breaking down dead wood and plants, while scorpions and centipedes patrol in search of food. Without these tiny invertebrates keeping nutrients cycling through the forest, the plants and large animals would not survive for long.

The spiny katydid of the Amazon rainforest is a prickly relative of crickets. Its spiny legs can discourage predators as large as bats and monkeys.

South-east Asia

South-east Asia has a mixture of rainforest and monsoon forest. People have cleared much of the land to grow crops such as rice, but lush forests survive on many islands and mountains.

Despite a fast rate of logging, Malaysia retains some patches of pristine forest, including those on the slopes of Mount Kinabalu in northern Borneo.

PAKISTAN INDIA [1] Himalayas
● Delhi
NEPAL

1. Himalayas
The highest mountain range in the world stops the moist monsoon air from reaching further into Asia and marks the northern edge of the tropical forest.

2. Sri Lanka
Much of the tropical forest that once covered this island has been cleared to make room for tea plantations.

3. Manas Sanctuary
The guards of this tiger sanctuary must constantly battle poachers.

4. Ujung Kulon National Park and Krakatau
This park protects Java's last large patch of forest, where the rare Javanese rhino lives. It also contains small islands, including the still-smoking cone of Anak Krakatau – son of Krakatau – a volcano that exploded in 1912.

5. Singapore
A city-state and important trade centre on an island off the Malaysian peninsula. It is occupied by some 4 million people from India, Malaysia, China and Europe.

Western Ghats

INDIA

N

[2] SRI LANKA

Sinharaja Forest Reserve

NORTH AMERICA EUROPE ASIA
AFRICA
SOUTH AMERICA AUSTRALIA
ANTARCTICA

Fact file

▲ South-east Asia lies at the meeting point of three of the plates that make up Earth's crust. The movements of these plates have created many mountains, volcanoes and islands.

▲ The coast in much of South-east Asia is covered with mangrove swamps – forests that grow in salt water.

▲ The main causes of deforestation in the region are logging for valuable hardwoods and forest clearance for farming or mining.

6. Angkor Wat
A world-famous complex of Hindu and Buddhist temples that rises from the jungle.

7. Cat Ba Island
This small and beautiful national park has diverse habitats, including evergreen rainforests, freshwater swamps and mangroves.

8. Gunung Mulu
Inside this mountain is a stunning set of limestone caves, including Earth's largest cavern. Over a million bats of many species roost here by day, before leaving at sunset to feast in the forest. The rich plant life in the park around the caves includes 3500 plant species, 109 of which are palm trees.

9. Kinabalu Park
Visitors like to climb through different kinds of forest to the top of Mount Kinabalu.

10. Maluku
Recently called the Moluccas, these islands were once called the Spice Islands, and spice crops are still grown there. Columbus was trying to reach these islands when he stumbled on the Americas.

Old man of the forest

Local people used to tell the story that orangutans were old men who had grown tired of living in villages and had left to lead a quiet life in the trees. In fact, they are apes that used to live all over South-east Asia, but they now survive only in patches of forest on the islands of Borneo and Sumatra. With few natural enemies, they grow and breed very slowly. In a lifetime of 45 years, a female orangutan has time to raise only four young, but each baby is cared for intensively. An orangutan mother carries her baby all the time during its first year, and only weans it onto solid food when it is three years old. She will not have another youngster for around eight years. At night, mother and baby sleep together in nests of woven branches.

People and tropical forests

From the hunter-gatherers of the past to the scientists of today, people have been making use of tropical forests for thousands of years.

The human race evolved in the tropics, so there probably have been people living in tropical forests for as long as our species has existed. The earliest archaeological evidence of settlements in a tropical forest comes from a cave in Sarawak, Malaysia, and dates back 40,000 years. The oldest evidence of people in South American forests is only 5000 years old, but that's not surprising. The human race did not reach the Americas until about 35,000 years ago, so there are fewer archaeological remains there.

Hunter-gatherers

We can never know for sure how people lived many thousands of years ago, but it's possible their way of life was similar to that of some modern forest peoples.

The Piaroa people of Venezuela still sometimes use blowpipes to hunt monkeys. The darts are tipped with paralyzing poison from the skin of frogs.

Most of the native peoples of the Amazon rainforest, for instance, lived until recent times in small communities of hunter-gatherers. Hunter-gatherers are people who collect and hunt their food from the wilderness, instead of growing crops.

A few people still live this way in remote parts of the Amazon, far from towns or roads. They hunt such animals as monkeys, deer, birds and even snakes. Today they often use guns for hunting, but in the past they used blowpipes, bows and arrows, nets or spears to catch their prey. Besides hunting for meat, they collect mushrooms and wild plant foods, such as fruit, nuts and swollen roots.

Coconut palms

The coconut palm is one of the most important crops in the tropics. Their seeds – coconuts – contain a milky drink and a rich, edible flesh, from which a valuable oil is extracted. The thick husks of coconuts yield coir – a very strong fibre used to make ropes, mats and brooms. The leaves of coconut palms are used for thatching and baskets, the leaf buds are eaten as a salad vegetable and the trunks are used to construct houses. The sugary sap from coconut flowers can even be made into an alcoholic drink called toddy.

Little people

Central Africa's Congo rainforest is home to three major groupings of people who live as hunter-gatherers: the Mbuti, Twa and Mbenga. These people have been called pygmies because they are very short. On average, they are only 1.2–1.42 metres (about 4 ft to 4 ft 8 in) tall.

The Mbuti, Twa and Mbenga hunt elephants and antelopes with small bows that fire poison arrows, and they also gather honey from bees' nests – a dangerous task, given the ferocious temperament of African

killer bees. Like the people of the Amazon, the people of the Congo's forest live in small communities and build temporary dwellings in the forest. There is no single leader in a community; instead members have general discussions to try and solve problems. Marriages are arranged between communities, forging family links that tie communities together. People can leave one community to join another whenever they like.

In common with other hunter-gatherer peoples, the Mbuti, Twa and Mbenga use the forest in a sustainable way. They live off its resources without having to fell the trees, so they do little damage to their environment.

The hunter-gatherer way of life is dying out in the Congo. The forest has been shrinking steadily for centuries because farmers from outside have been cutting down trees to grow crops. Increasingly, the Mbuti, Twa and Mbenga trade meat with their farming neighbours in exchange for knives, tools and crops like bananas, corn and rice.

Until about AD 900 people of the Mayan civilization built cities in the lowlands of Guatemala. Their temples now stand abandoned, overgrown by forest.

Beyond Africa

There are forest-living people in Sri Lanka and the Andaman Islands in the Indian Ocean who might be related to the forest people of the Congo. They look more African than Asian and are barely 1.5 metres (5 ft) tall. The Veddahs of Sri Lanka were probably the island's original inhabitants and have lived there for many thousands of years. More recent immigrants from India have since cut down much of Sri Lanka's forests, and the Veddahs are now a tiny group. Scientists believe that the Veddahs and other peoples living in isolated spots throughout the Indian Ocean are descendants of Africans who spread to Asia and Australia. Australia and New Guinea's aboriginal people are thought to belong to the same group.

Farming the tropics

Before the age of agriculture, most of the world's people lived as hunter-gatherers. At some point, however, people learned how to grow crops and raise their own animals. Since then, farming gradually spread around the world, and the hunter-gatherer way of life began to die out. Today, the last few hunter-gatherers live in tough environments where farming is difficult, such as deserts, arid (dry) savannas or the heart of dense rainforests.

In recent history, most cultures that have thrived in the tropics have lived by farming. To grow their food, farmers often had to clear the land of forest. In South-east Asia, for

Hunting animals is still an important feature of life on Fergusson Island, Papua New Guinea. This wild pig was caught in a trap.

instance, rice fields have taken the place of swampy rainforests in many areas. Most of India was once covered with monsoon forest, but today the bare landscape looks like an almost treeless grassland.

Colonial era

In the 15th century, European sailors began to explore the world. The driving force behind the expeditions was trade. European merchants knew that if they could travel to China and South-east Asia by sea, they could buy products such as silk and spices more cheaply than by overland routes, which were controlled by Persian and Arab traders.

To a European merchant, a tropical forest was nothing more than a place where spices grew. Spices such as nutmeg, pepper, cinnamon and cloves were important for cooking in those days because they masked the flavour of poorly preserved meat. But the Spice Islands (present-day Indonesia) were very far away. To get there, sailors had to make a perilous voyage all the way around

Jarawa

The Jarawa people live as hunter-gatherers in the rainforests of the Andaman Islands. They have lived in these forests for thousands of years, hunting wild pigs and monitor lizards, catching fish with bows and arrows and gathering seeds and berries. Their origins are unknown, but scientists think they may have come from Africa rather than Asia.

Today there are fewer than 400 Jarawa left on only two islands. Like other Andaman peoples, they are at risk of being relocated from their homeland by the Indian authorities, who want to 'civilize' (or just better control) them. Other peoples that have been moved have been almost wiped out by mainland diseases, such as measles. If the Jarawa are evicted from the forest, they are likely to share this fate.

The people of Papua New Guinea have used birds of paradise to make ceremonial headdresses for many generations, yet few of the birds are endangered. The main threat facing the island's wildlife is deforestation.

Africa, so they started looking for shortcuts. One such sailor was Christopher Columbus, who thought he could reach the Spice Islands by sailing west. He was wrong, but because of his mistake, Europeans came into contact with the Americas.

Going Dutch

By the 17th century, the Dutch controlled the production of spices in South-east Asia. They tried to restrict each spice to a single island – they grew nutmeg on one island, pepper on another and so on. They destroyed the spice trees on all other islands in the area to ensure they would get the highest price for their crop. However, their plan to monopolize the spice trade was foiled by

Attack of the Amazons

The first European to cross the Amazon rainforest was a Spanish explorer named Francisco de Orellana. In 1540, Orellana and a group of conquistadors marched across the Andes mountains east of Quito and reached a roaring waterfall leading to a wide river. They decided to build a sailing boat (which took weeks to construct) and send a group of men downriver to pick up supplies, with Orellana in charge. But Orellana never came back. By the time he found supplies, he had gone too far to turn around, and he faced attacks from hostile Indians. In one incident, his group was attacked by what appeared to be female warriors. The Spaniards called the mighty river down which they were sailing the Amazon, after the female warriors of Greek mythology, and the name stuck. It took them about a year to reach the Atlantic – a voyage of some 4750 km (3000 miles). After a stop in Trinidad, Orellana finally returned home to Spain.

Tea-pickers collect their harvest on a plantation in Sri Lanka. Only the tips – the youngest leaves – are picked. Tea grows best in places with a humid, rainy climate.

pigeons, which ate the fruits of spice trees and deposited seeds in their droppings on neighbouring islands.

By the start of the 20th century, most of the world's tropical forests were under European control, and colonists around the globe began to clear forests for plantations. Spices had already been introduced to Africa; cloves from Indonesia, for example, were being grown on the island of Zanzibar off the coast of Tanzania. Bananas, originally from Asia, were being grown in South America.

Far away, in northern Europe, the demand for forest products increased. Rubber, made from the resin of Amazon rubber trees, became a valuable commodity. As a result, rubber trees were soon growing in South-east Asia and on Pacific islands. The wealthy Europeans had also started drinking tea and coffee in large quantities, so tea and coffee plantations began to spread, as did plantations to grow sugar cane and cocoa.

Power to the people

Some of the world's largest cities are in the tropics, such as Bangkok in Thailand and São Paulo in Brazil. People have harnessed the heavy tropical rain to provide power for such cities. Hydroelectric power plants use water falling from a dam to generate electricity.

Natural rubber comes from the bark of a tropical tree native to Brazil. A sharp knife is used to cut the bark, then the rubber is collected in cups.

When people build a dam, the water trapped behind it forms a lake. Because many tropical rivers flow through flat land, dams built across them can flood vast areas of forest. The Amazon is the world's most dammed river, and it provides huge amounts of power to millions of Brazilians. However, the flooded forests that the dams create can be environmental disasters. The water kills plants and animals, and the dams stop fish and turtles from moving to their breeding grounds. The dead plants rot slowly in the water, releasing poisonous chemicals.

Forest products

In the past, people didn't think twice about cutting down a tropical forest to sell the timber or to farm the land to make money. Today, however, many people want to conserve tropical forests to protect the amazingly diverse wildlife. A good way to do this is to find a way of making the forest pay for itself.

There are several forest products that people can harvest without having to cut down the trees. Many are controlled by governments to make sure the forest wildlife is not damaged by over-zealous harvesting. For example, large leaves are collected from some tropical forests for use as packaging for gifts in the rich, industrial world. Similarly, the edible nests of cave-dwelling birds are collected in Borneo to make bird's nest soup in expensive Asian restaurants.

Chemical factories

The plants in tropical forests produce all sorts of poisonous chemicals that protect them from being eaten. Some of these chemicals could turn out to be useful drugs.

Many tropical plant chemicals are already used as drugs. The drug quinine, for instance, has long been used to treat malaria, the world's biggest killer disease. Quinine comes from the bark of the cinchona tree of South America, where people have been using it for centuries. When surgeons operate, they sometimes give patients a drug called curare to make their muscles relax. Curare comes from the roots of a South American vine. A more recent discovery was a plant called rosy periwinkle, which grows in the dry forests of Madagascar. It contains a drug that can help treat leukemia (cancer of the blood).

Scientists sometimes use local medicine men or witch doctors to help them find forest plants containing drugs. The witch doctors use many herbs in their healing ceremonies, and some of these could hold cures for AIDS or cancers. The wealth of drugs that might lie hidden in tropical forests makes it all the more important for us to protect them.

New Guinea

New Guinea is a rugged wilderness of mountains and rainforests. The western half is Irian Jaya, a province of Indonesia. The east is Papua New Guinea, an independent country.

Much of New Guinea is protected by the mountainous landscape, which makes the forest inaccessible to loggers. Waterfalls tumble off the steep slopes, such as this one near Tari in the Central Range highlands.

Birds of paradise

In the 16th century, Spanish sailors completed the first ever round-the-world trip. Among the exotic treasures they brought home were stuffed birds with such flamboyant feathers that they became known as birds of paradise. It was many years before scientists studied these birds in the wild, but they soon discovered that only the males sport bright colours, long tails and headdresses. They use their showy plumage to attract females in the gloom of the forest.

Fact file

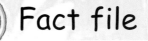

▲ More than two-thirds of New Guinea is cloaked in dense rainforest, sustained by the island's very high rainfall.

▲ The wildlife of New Guinea is more like that of Australia than South-east Asia. Most of the mammals are marsupials – mammals that carry their young in pouches.

▲ New Guinea is home to the cassowary, a large and dangerous flightless bird that can cripple or even kill a person with its powerful kick.

▲ Another unique inhabitant is the long-beaked echidna, a spine-covered mammal that lays eggs. The tip of its tongue has spikes for catching worms.

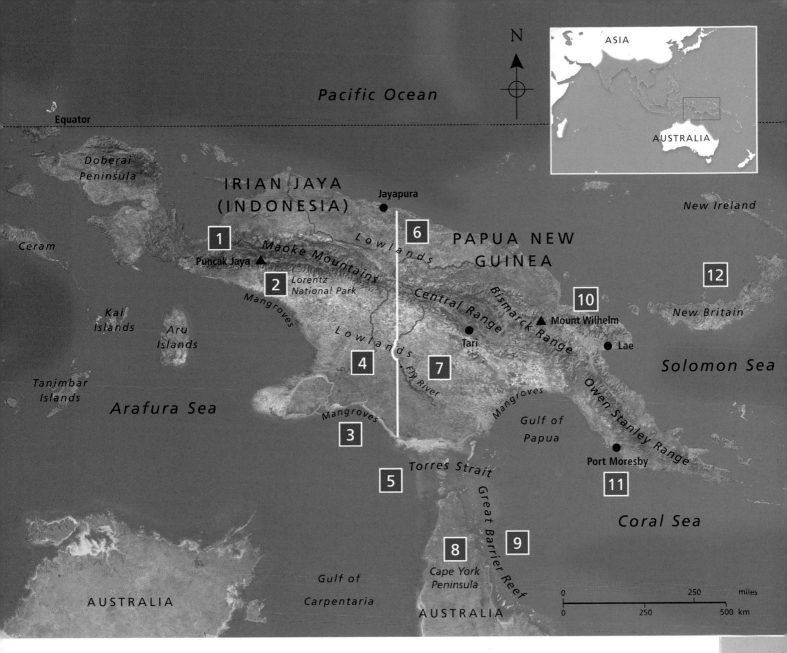

1. Puncak Jaya

The tallest mountain in New Guinea, with a peak of 5040 metres (16,535 ft). Unusually for tropical mountains, Puncak Jaya and its neighbours are snow-capped.

2. Lorentz National Park

The largest protected area in South-east Asia. It includes a range of tropical habitats, from snow-capped mountains to coastal wetlands.

3. Mangrove swamps

Dense mangrove swamps fringe the southern coast. New Guinea's mangrove swamps are as rich in tree species as mangrove swamps anywhere.

4. Southern lowlands

Freshwater swamp forests flourish in the lowlands. In scattered places are dense stands of klinki pines. These close relatives of monkey puzzles are the world's tallest tropical trees.

5. Torres Strait

New Guinea was joined to Australia until as recently as 8000 years ago, when rising seas flooded the Torres Strait.

6. Northern lowlands

The rainforests of northern New Guinea are home to Scott's tree kangaroo, New Guinea's largest and most endangered native mammal.

It has a strong smell that can linger for a week on a person who touches the animal.

7. Fly River

One of New Guinea's longest rivers, the Fly carries huge amounts of sediment washed off the steep mountains by heavy rain. The sediment provides nourishment for the coastal mangrove swamps.

8. Cape York Peninsula

Rainforest hugs the east coast of Cape York Peninsula, the most northerly part of Australia. The forest is home to numerous orchids and some of the same animal species as New Guinea, including two birds of paradise.

9. Great Barrier Reef

The northern tip of this vast system of coral reefs reaches up toward the Gulf of Papua.

10. Mount Wilhelm

The tallest mountain in Papua New Guinea, at 4509 metres (14,793 ft) high.

11. Port Moresby

The capital of Papua New Guinea and the largest city in New Guinea.

12. New Britain and New Ireland

Rain-drenched, forested islands forming part of Papua New Guinea. West New Britain gets 6 metres (20 ft) of rain a year.

The future

The world's tropical forests are disappearing rapidly, and many of their species are becoming extinct. Fortunately, there are lots of ways we can help protect the forests.

In 1850, the world's population was 1000 million or so; today it stands at over 6000 million. According to the United Nations, the world's population could more than double by 2050 if people keep having babies at the same rate. What does all this mean for the tropical forests of the world?

Many areas of tropical forest are in developing countries, where the population, though relatively low, is increasing fastest. Life can be difficult for people in developing countries. In some cases, people have little choice but to cut down the forests and use the land to raise cattle or grow crops. Every year, an area of tropical forest almost the size of Scotland is cut down by settlers who move to the forest to farm. If **deforestation** continues at this rate, the world's tropical forests could disappear in less than 100 years.

Starting point

Settlers were not the first people to start damaging the forest – loggers in search of huge hardwood trees came first. The best hardwoods are often exported to rich countries to make high-quality furniture,

? Ecotourism

One way to make a rainforest pay for its own protection is to invite paying tourists to take a holiday there. Tourists can now stay in floating hotels on the Amazon River or walk through the canopy of cloud forests in Costa Rica (right). People who go on such trips are called ecotourists, and the money they spend helps preserve the rainforest. Ecotourists have to follow strict rules to keep the environment healthy – after all, that's what they've come to see.

Commercial logging – both legal and illegal – is one of the biggest threats facing the Amazon rainforest.

but most timber from tropical forests is used for beams in houses across the world. Logging is a big business, worth £5000 million a year worldwide. A 1-metre (3-ft) cube of tropical hardwood can fetch more than £500.

Early loggers cleared large trees from the edges of forests. Later, logging companies began cutting roads into the forests to get at the huge trees in the interior. These roads let settlers move deeper into the forest to start farms, speeding up the deforestation.

Slash and burn

For thousands of years, people living in the forest have cleared small areas to use as vegetable gardens. The traditional way of doing this is to cut the trees down and burn them, a technique called slash and burn. The ash from the burned trees is rich in minerals and enriches the soil for a few years. But after three or four years, the minerals run out and the soil becomes poor. This happens very quickly in the tropics because the soil is thin and plants use up nutrients rapidly. So the farmer clears another patch of trees and lets the old land turn back into forest.

In recent times, settlers from outside the forest have used the same method on a much bigger scale. Because there are more mouths to feed, the settlers clear bigger areas and farm the land for as long as possible. Abandoned farms get reused after just a few years, instead of being left to revert to forest. This way of farming weakens the land so much that full tropical forest may not recover for centuries. Instead, patchy woodlands with small trees and dusty grasslands take its place.

Even where dense forest does grow back, it is secondary forest, with fewer species than the original primary forest.

Centuries of damage

When done carefully, logging does not cause a huge amount of damage to tropical forests and could be a good way of making money to protect them. Within a hundred years, the gap left by a felled tree fills up again, and only experts can tell that logging took place. However, clearing land for ranches or plantations can ruin it. Experts estimate that it would take the best part of 1000 years for tropical forests to grow back in such places.

Slash-and-burn agriculture (left) and floods created by dams (below) both contribute to deforestation in the Amazon. According to the government of Brazil, 14 per cent of Brazilian Amazon forest has been lost since 1970, and the rate of deforestation is speeding up.

Under threat

Impenetrable jungle and vast swamps once made most of the Amazon rainforest out of bounds to all but the most intrepid explorers or the resident population of native South Americans. Today, things are very different. Speedboats and new highways have opened up the region to developers, loggers, miners and farmers, and the landscape is changing fast. This map shows areas that still contain primary (undisturbed) rainforest (dark green) not currently threatened by destruction. The red zone is primary forest at high risk of deforestation and pale green is farmland and secondary forest – the impoverished forest that grows back after deforestation.

Primary forest not at immediate risk.

Primary forest threatened by deforestation.

Deforested land covered by farmland and secondary forest.

Pacific Ocean

Atlantic Ocean

N

Amazon Basin

SOUTH AMERICA

Even 1000 years might not be long enough for some stretches of deforested land. When a tropical forest is cut down, there is nothing to protect the thin soil from the sun, wind and pouring rain. The tropical sun turns the soil to dust, and heavy rain washes it away, leaving deep gashes in the countryside. This process, called **soil erosion**, can make the land look more like a desert than a jungle.

Changing climate

Just as the climate affects what grows in tropical forests, so the forest can affect the climate. Thick forests packed with trees release huge amounts of water that the plants have sucked up from the ground and given out through their leaves. The water vapour rising from the forest produces clouds, adding to the region's rainfall.

With the forest and the water vapour gone, there is less rain – and less cloud to shield the ground from the scorching sun. The once-rich soil turns into dust and blows away or bakes into a crust. Scientists have discovered

? Sustainable forests

Chopping down trees is not the only way to make money from a tropical forest. There are several ways the land can be used to grow food and other products without the forest being damaged beyond repair. The techniques currently being tested around the world are a mixture of new ideas and methods that have been used by local people for thousands of years.

Crops can be grown in combination with trees, which shade plants from the strong sun; coffee tastes even better when grown in the shade. Trees also provide support for vine crops, such as pepper and vanilla plants. Another way of conserving the forest is to plant a row of trees and shrubs around a field of crops. This green fence provides firewood, food for cattle and protects the crops from wind and sun.

Of course, it is also important to set aside areas where all farming, logging and other destructive practices are banned. These reserves are refuges for rare animals and plants, and they soak up rainwater, helping protect neighbouring areas from erosion.

that smoke from the fires started by slash-and-burn farmers can speed up this process by stopping rain clouds from forming.

Another climatic change caused in part by deforestation might be more far-reaching. When trees are cut down or burned, they release carbon dioxide – one of the gases that scientists think causes global warming. High in the **atmosphere**, carbon dioxide traps heat radiating from the ground, making the whole planet warm up. The process is called the greenhouse effect because it is similar to the way glass windows trap heat in a greenhouse. People have already released masses of carbon dioxide into the atmosphere by burning wood, coal, gas and oil; deforestation could make the problem worse.

Tapirs are famous for their ability to walk on riverbeds to escape from jaguars. These shy, short-sighted animals are dying out because of hunting and deforestation.

The Eden Project is a bold attempt to recreate an area of rainforest under a vast, dome-shaped greenhouse in England. Although such projects conserve few species, they help raise public awareness about deforestation.

Endangered species

Nobody knows how many species live in tropical forests, so nobody knows how many are being wiped out – but the answer is certainly a lot. You might wonder why it is so important to save species from extinction, given that there are plenty left. Many people believe that species are worth saving for their own sake – once a species is extinct, it is lost forever, making our planet a less interesting place. Another reason is that species rely on each other to survive. If we lose one, we will lose the species that depend on it, and so on – until one day little more than rats, cockroaches, weeds and humans remain.

The destruction of tropical forests is threatening some of the Earth's most beautiful animals, such as the tiger, the peculiar proboscis monkey, the timid aye-aye and the gentle tapir. These are just the species we know about – many more plants and insects are being destroyed before scientists get the chance to name them, before doctors can test them for medicines or before anyone can even look at them.

 # The golden lion tamarin

The stories of Brazil's tropical forests are not all bad. One that has a relatively happy ending is the story of the golden lion tamarin. This hamster-sized monkey is named for its luxurious golden fur and handsome mane. By the 1980s, its forest home on the coast of Brazil had almost disappeared, and the tamarin was on the verge of extinction. Its plight caught the attention of conservationists around the world, and a programme of breeding in zoos was started.

Tamarins raised in zoos across the world were soon being released into protected forests in Brazil. The first few monkeys had been raised in cages with branches fixed to the walls – they had never moved through a wild tree that swayed under their own weight. Tragically, most fell from the treetops to their deaths. From then on, conservationists made sure captive tamarins lived in trees, which helped them adjust to the wild after being released. Now, thanks to many years of hard work, golden lion tamarins have a chance to escape the threat of extinction.

Glossary

amphibian animal, such as a frog, toad or salamander, that lives partly in water and partly on land

atmosphere layer of air around the Earth

biome major division of the living world, distinguished by its climate and wildlife. Tundra, desert and temperate grassland are examples of biomes.

canopy roof-like layer of treetops in a dense forest

carbon dioxide gas released when fuel burns. Carbon dioxide is one of the main gases thought to cause global warming.

chlorophyll green chemical in the leaves and stems of plants that captures the energy in sunlight and helps convert it to food

climate pattern of weather that happens in one place during an average year

cloud forest type of tropical forest that grows on mountains and is often foggy or misty

cold-blooded having a body temperature that depends on the surroundings

deciduous describes a plant that sheds its leaves periodically

deforestation clearing of forest, usually carried out by cutting down or burning trees

equator imaginary line around the Earth, midway between the North and South Poles

epiphyte plant that grows on another plant and gets its water from the air or from rain

erosion gradual wearing away of land by the action of wind, rain, rivers, ice or the sea

evaporate to turn into gas. When water evaporates, it becomes an invisible part of the air

evolve to change gradually over many generations. All the world's species have formed through evolution.

fertile capable of sustaining plant growth. Farmers often try to make soil more fertile when growing crops.

hunter-gatherer person who obtains food by hunting, fishing and foraging rather than farming

infertile soil that is unable to support plentiful plant life is termed infertile

invertebrate animal that has no backbone, such as a worm, insect or spider

ivory hard white material that forms the tusks of elephants

mammal warm-blooded animal that feeds its young on milk. Mice, bats and whales are all mammals.

mangrove tree that grows in swamps on tropical coasts. Many mangroves have prop roots that support them.

marsupial type of mammal in which the young develop in a pouch on the mother's body

microclimate pattern of weather within a small area, such as a valley, treetop or burrow

monsoon very rainy season in South Asia; or the wind that causes the rainy season

nectar sugary liquid produced by a plant to attract the animals that pollinate its flowers

niche particular way of life and habitat of a species

nocturnal active at night

nutrient any chemical that nourishes plants or animals, helping them grow. Plants absorb nutrients from the soil, while animals get nutrients from food.

oxygen gas in the air. Animals and plants need to take in oxygen so their cells can release energy from food.

parasite organism that lives inside or on another organism and harms it

photosynthesis chemical process that plants use to make food from simple chemicals and the sun's energy

pollen dust-like powder made by the male parts of flowers

pollination transfer of pollen from the male part of a flower to the female part of the same flower or another flower

predator animal that catches and eats other animals

primate type of mammal that usually has grasping hands and forward-facing eyes. Most primates live in the trees of tropical forests.

rainforest lush forest that receives frequent heavy rainfall. Tropical rainforests grow in the tropics; temperate rainforests grow in cooler places.

reptile cold-blooded animal such as a snake, lizard, crocodile or turtle that usually has scaly skin and moves either on its belly or on short legs

savanna tropical grassland dotted with trees

sediment particles of sand or mud carried by a river

seed small, protective body containing a baby plant

soil erosion removal of soil from land by the action of wind and rain. Soil erosion often happens after deforestation.

species particular type of organism. Cheetahs are a species, for instance, but birds are not, because there are lots of different bird species.

swamp shallow wetland full of trees that can grow in water

temperate having a moderate climate. The temperate zones lie between the warm tropical regions and the cold polar regions.

tropic of Cancer imaginary line around the Earth 2600 km (1600 miles) north of the equator. There, the sun is directly overhead at noon on 21 June.

tropic of Capricorn imaginary line around the Earth about 2600 km (1600 miles) south of the equator

tropical between the tropics of Cancer and Capricorn. Tropical countries are warm all year.

tropical forest forest in the Earth's tropical zone, such as tropical rainforest or seasonal tropical forest

tropical grassland tropical biome that mainly contains grassland, such as savanna

venom poison injected by an animal using fangs or a sting

warm-blooded having a constantly warm body temperature. Mammals and birds are warm-blooded

Further research

Books

Attenborough, David. *The Private Life of Plants*. London: BBC Books, 1995.
Dunbar, Robin, and Barrett, Louise. *Cousins – Our Primate Relatives*. London: BBC, 2000.
Emmons, Louise. *Neotropical Rainforest Mammals: A Field Guide*. Chicago: University of Chicago Press, 1997.
Forsyth, Adrian, and Miyata, Ken. *Tropical Nature*. New York: Scribner, 1987.
Prance, Ghillean. *Rainforests of the World*. New York: The Harvill Press, 1998.
Whitmore, Timothy. *An Introduction to Tropical Forests*. London: Oxford University Press, 1998.

Websites

Wild World – Ecological Regions of the World: http://www.nationalgeographic.com/wildworld/terrestrial.html
(A huge resource from National Geographic and the Worldwide Fund for Nature. Through a clickable map, you can access pictures and profiles of 867 ecoregions, which are like smaller divisions of biomes.)
UNESCO World Heritage Sites: http://whc.unesco.org/nwhc/pages/sites/main.htm
(Includes descriptions of many of the world's most important tropical forest reserves.)
Rainforestweb: http://www.rainforestweb.org
(Links to sites about rainforest conservation.)
Passport to the Rainforest: http://www.passporttoknowledge.com/rainforest/main.html
(An interactive introduction to tropical rainforests.)

Index

Page numbers in *italics* refer to picture captions.

Picture credits

Key: l – left, r – right, m – middle, t – top, b – bottom. **Apex:** 60/61; **Ardea:** Jean Paul Ferrero 49t; Francois Gohier 44t; Nick Gordon 23b, 48, 58b; **Bruce Coleman:** 20; Alain Compost 7mr, 27; M.L.P. Fogden 9, 26b; Christer Fredriksson 23t; Luiz Claudio Marigo 10–11; Kim Taylor 16; Mark Taylor 21; Jorg and Petra Wegner 36t; Staffan Widstrand 18 (inset); Rod Williams 37b; **Corbis:** Karl Ammann 31; Tom Brakefield 33t; Michael and Patricia Fogden 45; Jeremy Homer 52; Wolfgang Kaehler 7r, 51, 54b; Bob Krist 53; Kevin R. Morris 7ml, 14; Kevin Schafer 22; Michael J. Yamashita 54t; **Image Bank:** Jean A.E.H. Duboisberranger 24; Darrell Gulin 6m, 17; Ted Mead 28–29; Jean-Pierre Pieuchot 10; Kevin Schafer 8, 56–57; Art Wolfe 34tl; **Lalangi Jayawardhana:** 49b; **NASA:** 12; **Nature PL:** Bruce Davidson 7l, 30; **NHPA:** G.I. Bernard 42t; Mark Bowler 42–43; James Carmichael Jr. 28t, 42b; Stephen Dalton 43t; Martin Harvey 34tr, 38t, 47, 60b; Daniel Heuclin 40b, 50; Mike Lane 61b; Andy Rouse 37t; Kevin Schafer 43b; Mirko Stelzner 32–33; Dave Watts 40t; Martin Wendler 57t, 58m; Norbert Wu 39t; **PhotoDisc:** Alan and Sandy Carey 38b, 41b; Geostock 41t; Robert Glusic 4m; Bruce Heinemann 5l; Jack Hollingsworth 5m; Photolink 5r, 11, 36t, 39t, 35; Stock Trek 12 (inset), 36b; Karl Weatherly 4r; **Popperfoto:** Reuters 16–17; **Science Photo Library:** Sinclair Stammers 44b; **Still Pictures:** Jacques Jangoux 46; Klein/Hubert 35b; Luiz Claudio Marigo 6r, 18, 39b; Michael Sewell 25. **Title page:** Image Bank, Ted Mead. **Front cover:** Bruce Coleman, Mark Taylor; NHPA, Andy Rouse (inset).